AWE-FILLED WONDER

The Interface of Science and Spirituality

BARBARA FIAND

**2008 Madeleva Lecture
in Spirituality**

PAULIST PRESS
New York/Mahwah, New Jersey

Book and cover design by Lynn Else

Library of Congress Cataloging-in-Publication Data

Fiand, Barbara.
    Awe-filled wonder : the interface of science and spirituality / Barbara Fiand.
        p. cm. — (2008 Madeleva lecture in spirituality)
        Includes bibliographical references.
        ISBN 978-0-8091-4529-4 (alk. paper)
        1. Spiritual life—Catholic Church. 2. Religion and science. I. Title.
        BX2350.3.F52 2008
        261.5′5—dc22

                                                        2007051131

Published by Paulist Press
997 Macarthur Boulevard
Mahwah, New Jersey 07430

www.paulistpress.com

Printed and bound in the
United States of America

Wonder AWE-FILLED WONDER **Awe-Filled**
Wonder Awe-Filled Wonder AWE-FILLED WON-
DER **Awe-Filled Wonder** Awe-Filled Wonder
AWE-FILLED WONDER **Awe-Filled Wonder**
Awe-Filled Wonder AWE-FILLED WONDER **Awe-**
Filled Wonder Awe-Filled Wonder AWE-FILLED
WONDER **Awe-Filled Wonder** Awe-Filled
Wonder AWE-FILLED WONDER **Awe-Filled**
Wonder Awe-Filled Wonder AWE-FILLED WON-
DER **Awe-Filled Wonder** Awe-Filled Wonder
AWE-FILLED WONDER **Awe-Filled Wonder**
Awe-Filled Wonder AWE-FILLED WONDER **Awe-**
Filled Wonder Awe-Filled Wonder AWE-FILLED
WONDER **Awe-Filled Wonder** Awe-Filled
Wonder AWE-FILLED WONDER **Awe-Filled**
Wonder Awe-Filled Wonder AWE-FILLED WON-
DER **Awe-Filled Wonder** Awe-Filled Wonder
AWE-FILLED WONDER **Awe-Filled Wonder**
Awe-Filled Wonder AWE-FILLED WONDER **Awe-**
Filled Wonder Awe-Filled Wonder AWE-FILLED
WONDER **Awe-Filled Wonder** Awe-Filled
Wonder AWE-FILLED WONDER **Awe-Filled**
Wonder Awe-Filled Wonder AWE-FILLED WON-
DER **Awe-Filled Wonder** Awe-Filled Wonder
AWE-FILLED WONDER **Awe-Filled Wonder**
Awe-Filled Wonder AWE-FILLED WONDER **Awe-**
Filled Wonder Awe-Filled Wonder AWE-FILLED

Barbara Fiand, PhD, is a Sister of Notre Dame de Namur. She teaches at the Institute of Pastoral Studies of Loyola University Chicago. She also gives retreats and lectures throughout the country and abroad on such issues as holistic spirituality, prayer, the influence of quantum discoveries on spirituality, and the transformation of consciousness. As people are faced today with a collapsing worldview, Dr. Fiand sees her primary work as helping them make the transition from the old and familiar to the new and sometimes frightening. She especially addresses concerns about how recent discoveries in physics affect traditional and often-treasured spiritual beliefs. She sees our time as an exciting opportunity for profound love and freedom.

Born in Indonesia of German parents, and originally a German citizen, Dr. Fiand now lives in Cincinnati. Her most recent book is *From Religion Back to Faith: A Journey of the Heart* (Crossroad, 2006). For Dr. Fiand's schedule of speaking engagements and her contact information, see her Web site at barbarafiand.com.

CONTENTS

PART II: REFOCUSING THE QUEST

Part I

*I*THE NTERFACE

1

SITUATING OURSELVES

Science does not need mysticism and mysticism does not need science; but [the human being] needs both.
—**Fritjof Capra**

We live in unparalleled times of transformation. Growth in human knowledge and the potential for expansion of consciousness have reached astounding proportions, unequaled in any other time of recorded history. We recognize today that we are interconnected not only with each other but, in fact, with all of reality. Scientific investigation and verification have shown us that what we do affects everything in the universe, just as every single event even in the farthest reaches of the cosmos affects us. These insights can be frightening, especially since the changes they call for, in our overall worldview as well as in our subsequent behavior, seem to be making demands on us with unforeseen and unsettling speed.

The discoveries of today can, however, also evoke hope and be accepted joyfully. They can, in fact, be seen as "gifting" us at this moment in the evolution of the universe and as graciously offering us the opportunity to become reconcilers and healers of our own human family that has been divided against itself and its environment for millennia and that has brought the planet on which it dwells into ever-more perilous straits.

Our global dilemma clearly is not news to anyone these days. It has been discussed numerous times both in the scholarly and popular literature of the day, as well as in films and television programs, especially during the last few years. The fundamental *why* of this dilemma and a possible solution are not as easily grasped. People generally are not intentionally ignorant and, as a wise friend of mine used to observe, "as a rule, do not do things that do not make sense to them." Rather, all of us tend to act within a framework of perception that appears sensible to us, if not always to others; that appears meaningful to us; and that—we often believe, not always correctly—appears generally accepted. Individuals do this, and cultures do this as well. What we today recognize as our perilous treatment of the earth and of each other came out of such a perspective, a paradigm of meaning that we used to interpret our place in the world of reality, our worldview, as it is most often referred to.

Scholars differ on the exact historical time frame of this worldview. Few would disagree, however, that it is now undergoing radical, even if not always welcome, transformation. Some see it as having emerged as far back as the agricultural revolution and the beginning of the patriarchal culture at the end of the Paleolithic era, when humans gradually began to experience themselves as separate from and superior to their environment and each other, and developed techniques of control and domination. Others point to the Hellenic period and the beginning of occidental philosophy, especially to the time of Plato and Aristotle when, among other intellectual speculations, formal principles of reality based on the experiences of change and the importance of, as well as the need for, permanence were identified and solidified. Still other scholars prefer to see this worldview emerging during the industrial revolution and the Enlightenment in the seventeenth and eighteenth centuries and beyond, when the age of reason brought us new tools for logical analysis and discursive thought, when the scientific method became normative, and when the mechanistic worldview became the overall umbrella for scientific self-understanding.

Dualism

I do not disagree with any of these views and, without meaning to make light of them, see them all as correct in one way or other. They focus on variations of an overall dualistic "atmosphere" and consequent world perspective, nuanced, to be sure, by a particular historical moment in which it found expression, but in which it lodged primarily and primordially in human collective consciousness. Dualism identified and defined reality in terms of its "natural" and observable dualities and differences. It focused on these dualities and differences, and absolutized these, stressing separation and "over-against-ness." It introduced into our awareness and interpretation of reality ever more-distinct categories of permanence and change, superiority and inferiority, inclusion and exclusion, spirit and matter, the sacred and the profane, the holy and unholy; and it soon pointed to one as good and its opposite as evil. In this way, for example, it fostered the rejection of spirit or of matter—depending quite arbitrarily on the mood of the times and the primacy of either "ism" (materialism or idealism-spiritualism) in any particular culture. In the last several centuries, it has been responsible for pitting the world of religion—the sacred—against the world of science, of modernity, of postmodernity and, in our own day, of anything that can no longer be easily explained by ancient, codified categories of thought and is, therefore, classified as New Age.

The dualistic worldview helped create the world we now inhabit, the culture whereby we live. It did so over centuries, even millennia, and today it is being challenged. Its demise, however, is in no way a smooth event, let alone an easy cultural transition. Marcus Borg describes culture well when he identifies it as "the socially constructed reality of a people, that nonmaterial 'canopy' of shared convictions which every human community erects and within which it lives....It consists of shared beliefs, values, meanings, laws, customs, institutions, rituals, and so forth, by which the group orders and maintains its world."[1] Culture is prized, cherished, and defended. Its constructs are seen as essential for the group's survival. It is, therefore, not something to be abandoned readily.

Our difficulty and pain in this regard are exacerbated by the fact that—although our cultural model, our worldview today, is being challenged, especially by the scientific discoveries of our time, and is therefore waning—our culture as a whole in many respects still understands itself dualistically. It thus depends for its operating assumptions on the perspective that has worked for it for thousands of years. If it is aware at all of the radically new revelations emerging today from the world of reality, it finds itself understandably defensive, resisting with force and denial, fearful of abandoning what has been its "truth" for millennia.

The Scientific Community

Even science, the actual birthplace of much that is new and radically different today, seems strangely prone to protecting itself from its onslaught. It has, after all, celebrated numerous "conquests" of the natural world under the umbrella of the dualistic/mechanistic model and, consequently, is loath to abandon it. Though most of the transforming insights of today come from daring pioneers in the scientific community, these pioneers frequently discover they are outcasts when they first identify their findings. Only years and many hardships later, when the evidence for their discoveries can no longer be refuted, do some of them get access again to the official scientific fold.[2]

Similar to various Christian religions, the academy of science has its own "central dogmas," as Bruce Lipton calls them.[3] For science, these are based on a materialistic, mechanistic view of reality and are in stark opposition to religion, which stresses the primacy of spirit. However, for both science and religion, their respective dogmas are firmly rooted in the great divide of dualism, and it takes courage and passion—the persistence of pioneer explorers and visionaries on both sides—to venture past its boundaries.

Our Task

The topic for this 2008 Madeleva lecture invites us to join these pioneers and visionaries, to experience with them the awe-filled wonder of the *new* that is unfolding in our time, and to seek the interface of science and spirituality. We will try to do so with simplicity, integrity, and honesty. As you know, the primary interest of this lecture series is spirituality. I am not a scientist and do not pretend to understand the intricacies of scientific formulations. I have the deepest respect for these, but my interest lies primarily in the end-product of scientific research: the discoveries, insights, and theories that it can offer us today in our quest for ultimate meaning and for a better world. I want to explore some of these with you during this lecture.

It would be nice, of course, if we could start our reflections on this topic with a generally accepted premise that there is indeed a connection, an interface, between science and spirituality. The preceding introductory discussion was intended, however, as a warning: matters are not as easy as that. Not long ago I received an e-mail from a gentleman unknown to me who informed me that he had purchased my book *Wrestling with God* in a used bookstore for the sum of one dollar. He wanted me to know that he had bought the book in order to bring it to a gathering of concerned Catholics who regularly burn books that should be on the

"Index"—a venerable, in his view, but discontinued practice of our tradition. He told me he would burn my book at this gathering and then he suggested a reliable exorcist for me. *Wrestling with God* was one of the first books in which I tried to relate scientific insights to religious issues.

Recognizing the significance of science for religion is a new phenomenon in our time and speaks against years of mutual disregard and even enmity. Galileo was perhaps its most famous victim. He was tried for heresy by the Inquisition, put under house arrest, and ordered to recant, while on his knees, his support for Copernicus's observation that the earth rotates around the sun and is not, as religion maintained at that time, the center of the universe. His less-known predecessor, monk and philosopher Giordano Bruno, was treated even less kindly. He was burned at the stake for declaring the same. The new and unfamiliar can be terribly frightening, and fear can drive us to violence.

Our integrity, however, mandates that we face life courageously come what may; that we do so with open eyes and open hearts out of reverence for the ultimate mystery unfolding there. Revelation, I suggest, did not end with the last writings of the Christian Scriptures in the first century. It has been an ongoing process throughout the centuries of human longing for the Holy. Today, perhaps more than at any other time in history, we know that no discipline is exempt from this depth quest; that all authentic knowing enriches us, empowers us as a human family, and is meant for us all. Nothing is too secular or too sacred for our sojourn on this earth, given to us for safekeeping.

2

MOMENTS OF REVELATION

I want to know how the Old One thinks. The rest is a detail.
—**Albert Einstein**

Reflections on the interface of science and spirituality can happen at various levels of sophistication. My hope, as I stated earlier, is to do so with as little complication as possible: to identify the discoveries and theories of science briefly and as simply as I am able in order to let them help us— free us up, if you will—to address concerns in Christian spirituality that have long appeared to me in need of reflection and possible re-visioning.

The above citation from Einstein is perhaps a good starting point. As is well known, Einstein resisted being identified with religion proper. He did not see membership in a particular faith-system as necessary for belief in God and resented having himself branded an atheist because of that. He is said to have had very definite categories of interpretation in his approaches both to ultimate meaning, as well as to his own area of scientific research. He is also known to have rejected even some of his own most extraordinary discoveries pointing him, as they did, to a post-Newtonian, postmechanistic, and radically new worldview.

The Expanding Universe

In 1914, through the mathematical symbols Einstein had scribbled on a sheet of paper in front of him, "the universe," as Brian Swimme expressed so well, "whispered that it was expanding in all directions." Through Einstein, we might say, the universe announced *that it was expanding*. The universe explained itself, in other words, not in Newtonian terms as "unchanging infinite space…a celestial container that housed the stars and planets and everything else" including us, but as having "erupted as a single ultimate density of being fifteen billion years ago."[4] Einstein, we are told, was shocked. He could not bear the shattering effect such a revelation would have on the prevailing worldview of his time and altered his equations, trying desperately to preserve the well-established scientific "dogma" of an unchanging universe. He fiercely denied his own findings until finally in the 1920s Edwin Hubble's telescope irrevocably confirmed what is now known as Einstein's general theory of relativity.[5]

Einstein's discovery strangely places us, once again, at the center of the universe. This, however, can no longer be viewed as a unique place of static prominence, as it had been once for largely religious reasons (geocentrism). The center of the universe as well as its birthplace are, in fact, everywhere at once. Today we know that we live in "an omni-centric evolutionary universe, a developing reality which, from the beginning, is centered upon itself at each place of its existence. In this universe of ours to be in existence is to be at the cosmic center of the complexifying whole."[6] We cannot distance ourselves from it or find ourselves somehow outside the expansion either in terms of time or space, objectively able to observe the event. We are, rather, deeply inside this process. We belong to it, are part of it, and are held in it, expressing it at every moment. "Even our thoughts about this process are simply yet another interesting current of micro-events taking place inside the great macro-event of the fifteen-billion-year development."[7] And, as the universe becomes ever larger, space "happens," is created, bursts forth between the galactic clusters in the event of expansion, driving galactic clusters ever farther apart.[8]

Seeking the Ground of Being

Clearly, the question to be answered, as we attempt to fathom all of this, is how it is even possible. Where does the energy, the power, come from that allows this event to be? If there is no "outside" that "influences," that brings forth what is, how does it happen? Theories and language attempting to respond to this question vary, though the notion of an underlying, supporting, and empowering "Field" (quantum field, zero-point field, akashic field, morphogenetic field) seems to be the most frequently referred to explanation offered by the various scientist-pioneers in physics and related areas of research.

What is perhaps most pressing for nonscientists, who are often unconsciously still part of a Newtonian worldview yet trying to open themselves up to these revolutionary insights, is the need to come to grips with the concept of *pure vacuum,* with a non-visible, pure emptiness characterizing this "Field" and mysteriously, as well as paradoxically, giving rise to everything that is, by way of interaction and annihilation. From it, reality is said to flare forth into newness by the creation and destruction of subatomic particles bursting into existence and vanishing, only to burst forth anew again and again. "Such creative and destructive activity takes place everywhere and at all times throughout the universe."[9] It generates newness (creative birth, death, and rebirth) in the farthest regions beyond the galaxies in what appears to be only a void, as well as in the tiniest gaps within our very brain. Pure vacuum is omnipresent. The Buddhist concept of *shunyata,* seeing space as "empty and yet full of potential," is perhaps the closest any spiritual insight has come to addressing it. Brian Swimme calls it an "empty fullness, a fecund nothingness." It is the ground of the universe—not, as was previously thought, inert matter, but seething, rather, "with creativity, so much so that physicists refer to [its] ground state as 'space-time foam.'"[10]

Lynne McTaggart, struggling with this concept and trying to make it simple for us, refers to it as the zero-point field (a name given to it by quantum physics). "What we tend to think of as a sheer void if all of space were emptied of matter and energy...is, in subatomic terms, a hive of activity," she tells us. Due to "a ground state field of energy constantly interacting with all subatomic matter," no particle is ever completely at rest. "The basic substructure of the universe is a sea of quantum fields." These are best understood as regions of influence held in the zero-point field as their repository and "cannot be eliminated by any known laws of physics." What appears to us as a "stable, static universe is in fact a seething maelstrom of subatomic particles fleetingly popping in and out of existence,"[11] which, cumulatively across the universe, give rise to enormous energy, believed to be "more than is contained in all the matter in the world"[12] by a factor of 10 to the fortieth power (1 followed by 40 zeros).[13]

We live in and breathe "what amounts to a sea of motion—a quantum sea of light."[14] In this world the exchange of energy in constant redistribution is the intrinsic property of all that is, of every particle—transient and insubstantial in itself, and incapable of separation from the fundamental reality underlying everything: the zero-point field.

> But there [is] also a larger implication of a vast underlying sea of energy. The existence of the Zero Point Field [implies] that all matter in the universe [is] interconnected by waves, which are spread out through time and space and can carry on to infinity, tying one part of the universe to every other part. The idea of the Field might just offer a scientific explanation for many metaphysical notions, such as the Chinese belief in the life force, or qi, described in ancient texts as something akin to an energy field. It even [echoes] the Old Testament's account of God's first dictum: "Let there be light," out of which matter was created.[15]

Metaphors for God

For many of us, these insights of scientific pioneering can be overwhelming as well as unsettling. They seem to invite us to venture far beyond accepted tradition were we to attempt to apply them to spirituality in general or even to our own personal reflections concerning ultimate Mystery. Once, however, we overcome our fear of stepping beyond the established boundaries of traditional science—as well as beyond those set up by organized religion and based, often unconsciously, on ancient scientific worldviews—the sense of mystery and awe inspired by these insights and discoveries can be most rewarding.

It is a fact often overlooked, especially by those who proclaim *their* view of God as the only valid one: *Everything* that at any time in human history has ever been spoken about God—

a) in *any* religion,
b) *outside of* formal religion, and
c) even *before* the formulations of organized religion,

everything that *can* in fact, be spoken about God, even by the most inspired mystic—is *metaphor*. Symbolic expression is the primary articulation of religious experience. It cannot be otherwise, by virtue of our very nature as finite beings and the nature of the divine Mystery that far surpasses our understanding. The metaphors that we choose, furthermore, are clearly selected, have at all times been selected, and will continue to be selected, according to the culture and context in which we live. All God-talk is contextual. As the context changes, religious expressions also change or, at least, *should* change for the sake of cultural relevance, in order to continue to foster the connection with the Holy for which they are intended.

The difficulty within Christianity, especially Catholicism, lies in our Greco-Roman heritage and its insistence on ownership of *unchanging* and *eternal* truths. When something is declared infallible (therefore, as eternal truth) to the entire church and with an "anathema" warning for anyone who does not accept it, it becomes difficult even for serious, adult believers to introduce change or to at least invite reexamination. The finalization of Christian dogma, especially in the fourth century and then throughout the centuries that followed, allowed for little variations. Even today anyone who dares to rethink the symbols and metaphors of our faith for the sake of relevance does so with trepidation.[16]

Yet the God who emerges when we give ourselves to a serious consideration of the findings of science (physics, biology, cosmology, human developmental, experimental psychology, and so on) no longer comfortably fits many of the models of our tradition. We can, of course, choose a kind of intellectual and religious dissonance—that is, study the new revelations from science but refuse to apply any of these to our spiritual quest. Much of that has happened in the past in the name of "faithfulness" to the literal teachings of Holy Scripture. Alternatively, we can choose the less-traveled road, take the risk, and allow ourselves to embrace the awe and wonder that surely will gift us when we honestly face what is offering itself to us in our day. We can then venture forth with authentic respect for, and loyalty to, our tradition, while at the same time look for what may graciously surprise us with newness and life.

Adjusting Our God Space

Given what we have reflected on so far, it would seem that the God of today no longer can be seen as *external* to the world, as above us: a God divorced from reality and working on it like the craftsman of old who rested on the seventh day when creation was finished, or even like the divine clockmaker of the Enlightenment. Creation, as we understand it today, is an ongoing, evolutionary event bursting forth from the center of the universe and continuing to expand in ever-new and extraordinary ways. God, we might say, expresses God's power *there* and emerges *within it*. In an omnicentric universe we, and everything else with us, are at its center and, amazingly, at all times at its beginning as well. As strange and paradoxical as this may seem to the linear time-and-space categories of our mind, what it implies is that the creative energy of this universe is held in each of us.

 God operates in us and ever flows through us, energizes us, and can never be separated from us.

Concepts of God, then, as a humanlike generator of life—a father or mother, or a judge sitting on a throne above and "seeing" everything we do, punishing us by "separating" us from "himself," or rewarding us by drawing us "near"—are foreign and seem misplaced in a "sea of quantum fields," an omnicentric "space-time foam" of creativity.

More specifically, our Christian imagery of heaven as "above"—a place *from which* God descends, a place *to which* Jesus ascended after the resurrection, and a place *into which* Mary was assumed at her death—no longer fits into religious imagination based on the emerging world perspective. Envisioning Jesus, then, as sitting at God's right hand and coming from above in glory at the end of time to judge all of us, who will then be returned to our former embodiment, will, among other things, demand some serious "de-literalization."

These religious interpretations fit well into an understanding of a static universe with the earth as a plate and heaven as a dome covering it. They fit into a linear space/time frame with a beginning and an end of time, and with space as a fixed place extended in measurable directions. An anthropomorphized version of God belonged there, and our being made "in God's image" took on physical characteristics. Ironically, this interpretation was really upside down: we made God in *our* image instead—with hands to hold us, feet to walk in the garden, and eyes to watch us; with a definite gender capable of impregnating a virgin; and with all the emotions of anger, vengeance, and jealousy, and the subsequent behaviors associated with human beings and projected onto the divine. Even the notions of eternity and infinity were reduced to a "no end" and "no beginning" of what *we* experience as linear spatial and temporal concepts.

Lessons Learned from Light

We know today from research into the nature of light that time and space are relative. As Peter Russell, a physicist and student of consciousness, tells us: "For an observer actually traveling at the speed of light, the equations of special relativity predict that time would come to a complete standstill, and length would shrink to nothing."[17] Light, of course, travels at the speed of light. From its own perspective, therefore (if one could speak this way), it "travels no distance and takes zero time to do so."[18] This transcendence of space and time reveals something strange, indeed.

 "Whatever light is, it seems to exist in a realm where there is no before and after. There is only now,"[19] and only the here.

For us and for our commonsense appreciation of reality, this is incomprehensible, for we are used to seeing space and time as constants. For some people, as mentioned before, these constants even spill over into eternity where it is expected (dogmatically declared, in fact) that our actual bodies will find a *place* of rest. Others will find a place of punishment, of course, or of expiation. It is difficult for us to accept that the spatial and temporal dimensions we live in and take for granted are merely categories of our mind. We find it absurd to think of them as simply relative—as forms, in other words, of our particular mode of consciousness, not independent of it, but created by it and nonapplicable in other realms of reality. But the study of light assures us that they are precisely that.

Science today agrees with the philosopher Emmanuel Kant, who insisted already in the eighteenth century that we cannot see the world other than in spatial and temporal categories. "The human mind is so constituted that it is forced to construct its experience within the framework of space and time," Kant maintained. These, however, are not "fundamental dimensions of the underlying reality. They are fundamental dimensions of consciousness,"[20] that is, categories of reason.

Wisdom of Scientists and Mystics

The physicist Erwin Schrödinger observes bluntly: "Every [person's] world picture is and always remains a construct of his [or her] mind, and cannot be proved to have any other existence."[21] Mystics from both East and West have, of course, generally experienced this fact, and advised us not to confuse *our* reality with *the* reality—Ultimate Reality, which, in fact, ever remains Mystery.

Kant called this ultimate reality the *noumenon*. Brian Swimme refers to it, among other things, as the "unseen ocean of potential…an infinity of pure generative power."[22] Ervin Laszlo speaks of what is also called the *quantum vacuum* as "the energy- and information-filled plenum that underlies our universe, and all universes in the Metaverse."[23] Along with physicist David Bohm, Laszlo understands *information* not as "a human artifact, not something that we produce by writing, calculating, speaking, and messaging," but rather, "as ancient sages knew, and as scientists are now discovering, *information* is produced by the real world and is conveyed by a fundamental field that is present throughout nature." It extends far beyond individuals or even the entire human race and is an "inherent aspect of nature" itself.[24] David Bohm named it the "implicate order." As Michael Talbot explains, Bohm had a holographic view of the universe, which he identified as a dynamic and ever-active "holomovement." Underlying our perceived reality, "a deeper order of existence, a vast and more primary level of reality… gives birth to all the objects and appearances of our physical world in much the same way that a piece of holographic film gives birth to a holo-gram."[25] Our existence is an *unfolding* of this implicate order in a continuous universe-wide process of bringing forth *(explicating)* and return-ing once again *(enfolding)* into the implicate order.[26] Bohm sees this process as a "disappear-ing" back into the "abyss" of the implicate order followed by a "re-emergence" rather than a literal annihilation and rebirth process.[27]

Of particular interest to the topic of this lecture, and somewhat similar to Brian Swimme's view, is the perspective of John Hegelin, a professor of physics. He was interviewed by the producers of the film *What the Bleep!? Down the Rabbit Hole: One Movie. Infinite Possibilities.* Hegelin spoke of this mysterious, dynamic, ultimate reality as the "unified field of *pure consciousness*," as pure being where everything has its source, as an ocean of being at the basis of existence, as pure potentiality that is the nonmaterial unifying field of conscious-ness, the fountainhead of all laws of nature and everything in it. It percolates up through our phys-iology, he tells us, into what we see and experience.

Russell supports Hagelin's observations by maintaining that, contrary to the materialist para-digm still prevalent today, "consciousness does not arise from some particular arrangement of nerve cells or processes going on between them, or from any other physical features; *it is always present.*"[28] It manifests itself through our individuality. We encounter what *is*, according to our human mode of awareness, which is different from that of other beings such as animals and even plants.[29] The unique form by which consciousness expresses itself in us gives rise to the colors we see and the sounds we hear in the "external world," while actually there is only light at various frequencies calling for our specific response of sight, and only pressure waves in the air that we receive as sound.[30] Matter (generally taken for granted by us as real just the way we encounter it) is also actually a construct of our particular consciousness. Matter is, in fact, 99.9 percent emptiness. We, however, experience it as solid. This, Russell explains, is largely so because of the rapidity of subatomic particles spinning around their nucleus.[31]

According to Hagelin, the unified field of pure consciousness (what McTaggart interestingly referred to as the "quantum sea of Light") holds all and transcends the division between mind and matter. Our specific form of receiving reality through the filter of our nervous system individualizes and categorizes pure consciousness according to our needs.

 At the base, however, all is one—nonmaterial, dynamic, self-aware intelligence. Truly knowing this through experience, Hagelin maintains, is enlightenment.

This experience transcends religion, he insists. It is nonsectarian and can be taught to all who truly seek. Brian Swimme affirms this insight. Speaking from the point of view of cosmology, he observes:

The importance of the cosmological tradition is its power to awaken those deep convictions necessary for wisdom. Knowledge of all-nourishing abyss is the beginning of a process that reaches its fulfillment in direct taste. We think long and hard about such matters as a way of preparing ourselves for tasting and feeling the depths of a reality that was always present and yet so subtle it escaped us.

It may be that in the next millennium religious convictions will be awakened and established within the young primarily by such meaningful encounters with the mysteries of the universe, and only secondarily by the study of sacred scriptures. The task of education then will focus on learning how to "read" the universe so that one might enter and inhabit the universe as a communion event.[32]

3

SPIRITUAL CHALLENGES

*Affairs are now soul size. The enterprise
is exploration into God.*
                        —Christopher Fry

Call to Transformation

It is clear that these profound encounters with
the cosmos, and with everything that gifts us
deep within its unfolding, will necessitate major
transformation in our current fact, speed, and
content-oriented educational models. Hagelin's
"enlightenment" rarely if ever happens without
the patient waiting and listening that comes with
meditation and with the surrender of personal
ambition, need for control, and drive to compete.
Swimme's "communion event" demands, above
all, the letting-go of individualistic interests in
favor of deeper treasures.

Christian philosopher and spiritual writer
Beatrice Bruteau agrees with this. She tells us that
communion, in the Teilhardian sense, is the cre-

ative, driving force behind evolution itself, and its depth energy is love. Self-surrender and subsequent union for the sake of greater complexity have been the evolutionary story of the universe from its beginning. Teilhard believed that this story is now, in and through humanity as the uniting element, moving toward full recognition, toward conscious and free expression. We might say that, in us, this cosmic "love story of union toward greater consciousness" longs to express itself in total awareness, in a universal, all embracive *yes* that allows for full realization. Teilhard sees this as crucial for the next evolutionary moment and claims that "the whole cosmic enterprise now hangs on our decision." In that sense, in fact, *"we are evolution."*[33]

Of course, because of our inherent freedom, each one of us can still choose whether we will embrace communion with one another and all of creation, whether the insights that gift us at this time in history will draw us together, or whether we will stubbornly deny our destiny. There is then the possibility for

a genuine choice *for* community, a sincere acceptance of the family of creation. The love that Teilhard talks about as the power for community drives us beyond our individualism to unite toward what evolution requests of us. Our *yes* to this love is what he sees as *our* step toward the fulfillment of all things in Christ; for the community we are asked to build will subsume and embrace everything that has gone before, and all of creation will be blessed.[34]

 It took a genius such as Einstein for the universe to bring its omnicentricity to full awareness. It will take no less then all of us for the universe to reveal its primal energy as love.

Limitations of Science as *Science*

For all of us, I believe, the challenges presented here can be both exciting and unnerving. Certainly, from the Christian perspective, one of the first concerns highlighted by scientific theories and discoveries of the sort we have been reflecting on would be about the seeming lack of room for a *personal* God. We will return to this later in our reflection. For the moment we might allow ourselves to be reassured somewhat at least by recalling that, for a very long time and only until recently (with the major exception of Teilhard de Chardin who was both mystic *and* scientist and considered the arenas of both science and religion as *holy ground*), God was given no place at all in scientific research. It seems fascinating, therefore, that the mystery encountered by science today, pointing as it does to a non-visible underlying source (regardless of the name given to it and hypotheses surrounding it), hints somehow at a spiritual reality after all, even

30

if not consciously claimed as such. It seems to signal a return of one kind or another to the inescapable Holy pervading all.

Aniella Jaffé in her little book *The Myth of Meaning* supports this observation by citing a number of scientists of the mid-twentieth century. Lincoln Barnett observes:

> In exploring the macrocosm [one] comes at last to a final featureless unity of space-time, mass-energy, matter-field—an ultimate, undiversified, eternal ground beyond which there appears to be nowhere to progress....[One] finds barriers on every side and can perhaps but marvel, as St. Paul did nineteen hundred years ago, that "the world was created by the word of God so that what is seen was made out of things that do not appear."

Jaffé points to what she calls "the religious echo" in this observation by James Jeans: "The spirit no longer appears to us an intruder in the realm of matter; we begin to suspect that we should rather welcome it." Jaffé also mentions W. Heitler's "postulate of an autonomous and regulating 'spiritual principle,'" as well as A. Portmann's "concept of an invisible 'abyss of mystery,' containing the structural elements of life, of an 'immense, unknown realm of the mysterious.'"[35] She sees all these observations as coming close to the religious and spiritual realm.

It would seem that science today points to the mystery but admits that, *within the limits of its own discipline,* it can go no further. Arthur Stanley Eddington articulates this fact clearly:

> We have learnt that the exploration of the external world by the methods of physical science leads not to a concrete reality but to a shadow world of symbols, beneath which those methods are unadapted for penetrating. Feeling that there must be more behind, we return to our starting point in *human consciousness*—the one center where more might become known. There [in immediate inward consciousness] we find other stirrings, other revelations than those conditioned by the world of symbols....Physics most strongly insists that its methods do not penetrate behind the symbolism. Surely then that mental and spiritual nature of ourselves, known in our minds by an intimate contact transcending the methods of physics, supplies just that...which science is admittedly unable to give.[36]

Nevertheless, some scientists do move beyond the boundaries of their discipline and reach for the mystery without apology. This seems to be true both of Fritjof Capra *(The Tao of Physics)* and Peter Russell *(From Science to God).* Others, like most of those cited above, stay within—allow themselves to come so far, but ultimately shy away from openly religious claims.[37] Their task, they explain, is to deal "with shadows, not reality," shadows that, as in Plato's allegory of the cave, point beyond but cannot do more. What is *new* in the "new" physics is that its scientists now actually *know and acknowledge* this. "The new physics was forced to be aware of that fact,"[38] says Ken Wilber.

"Unknowing"

What is exciting to me about this awareness and subsequent acknowledgment by some scientists today is the fact that the admission of human finitude in the face of the "More" is itself already a deeply spiritual act, and perhaps in *that* is science's greatest wisdom and its deepest spiritual connection. The shadows discovered by science point to depth reality. Scientists today admit this but stand silent in its presence, knowing that, as scientists, they do not have the wherewithal to apprehend it *in itself*. This shift in the new science is extraordinary. It is, indeed, a move from the previously reductionistic:

> It is not visible, cannot be measured, is not empirically verifiable, and, therefore, does not exist;

to the open-ended:

> It is non-visible, non-visualizable even. It defies measurability, time and space, and, yet, its exis-

*tence, though beyond our expertise to know, can-
not be denied.*

There is an experiential quality to the mystical,
an extraordinary encounter, of one kind or another,
with the Holy. As we have discussed above, scientists tell us that this lies outside their discipline.
Scientists *as* scientists claim neither experience nor
competence discussing depth reality. I wonder
whether, perhaps as one possible step toward
mutual support and an authentic interface, religion
might not do well if it allowed itself to seriously
reflect on and possibly even embrace some of science's honesty and humility in this regard. Religious
declarations about the nature of the Holy, though
they are obviously not expressed in mathematical
symbols, are nevertheless always and unquestionably metaphoric statements of faith. They are contextual in nature and, therefore, at all times
tentative. Does not the interface, then, ultimately
begin for both disciplines in "unknowing," rather
than in fooling ourselves with rational certitudes?

The mystical experience of, and response to,
Holy Mystery seems to lead the way here. It makes
no attempts at explaining or justifying itself.
Though it is often rooted in a religious tradition,
it frequently surpasses that tradition's understanding of the Holy. It speaks its experiences with can-
dor and directness even if they are puzzling, even
if they frequently seem paradoxical, and even if

they can appear contrary to accepted beliefs. As a result, the mystical can threaten those who need to have definite and final answers. It has, therefore, a history of rejection, ridicule, and even persecution. In many respects, however, the mystic's experience, because of its directness, can point and more readily give expression to the unfathomable that science is now encountering.

As an aside, but nevertheless of possible interest in this regard, my own study of the phenomenology of atheism, be it scientific or philosophical in origin, led me already in my early teaching years to surmise that it was not the mystical response *as such* to the all embracive Mystery that was rejected by some of the most famous atheists of the past. Russell's insights are telling here:

> When we consider the writings of great saints and sages, we do not find many claims for God being in the realm of space, time, and matter. When they talk of God—the Holy Spirit, the Divine Light, the Beloved, Yahweh, Elohim, Brahman, Buddha nature, the Being behind all creation—they are usually referring to a profound personal experience. When we want to find God, we have to look within, into *deep mind*—a realm that Western science has yet to explore.[39]

The god rejected by atheists was most often not the one encountered in "deep mind," but rather a literalized "image" of God held up as absolute—a god defined and codified by declarations of certitude, devoid of depth and of the awe-filled Mystery that whispers to us of the truly Holy.[40] Absolute certainty seems out of place to me in all religious language, for religion, in the final analysis, also sees merely "through a glass darkly." When it forgets this, it destroys its purpose and serves only itself.

 The meeting point, then, of science and religion is humility, honesty, trust, and a common passion for the yet unknown.

Scientists beyond Science

Now, as we turn once again to the topic of science and ponder its findings, we discover that, in spite of the acknowledged limitations with respect to spiritual matters inherent in this discipline, the insights scientists *can* point to and open up for all of us as "seekers of the More" can actually be quite extraordinary. Above all in these times, science can help *contextualize* our encounter with the Sacred in entirely new ways and can thus reveal horizons of depth hitherto unknown. Fritjof Capra says in his preface to *The Tao of Physics:*

I was sitting by the ocean one late afternoon, watching the waves rolling in and feeling the rhythm of my breathing, when I suddenly became aware of my whole environment as being engaged in a gigantic cosmic dance. Being a physicist, I knew that the sand, rock, water, and air around me were made of vibrating molecules and atoms, and that these consisted of particles which inter-acted with one another....I knew also that the earth's atmosphere was continually bombarded by showers of "cosmic rays," particles of high energy undergoing multiple collisions as they pen-etrated the air. All this was familiar to me from my research in high-energy physics, but until that moment I had only experienced it through graphs, diagrams, and mathematical theories. As I sat on that beach, my former experiences came to life; I "saw" cascades of energy coming down from outer space, in which particles were created and destroyed in rhythmic pulses; I "saw" the atoms of the elements and those of my body participat-ing in this cosmic dance of energy; I felt its rhythm and I "heard" its sound, and at that moment I *knew* that this was the Dance of Shiva, the Lord of the Dancers worshipped by the Hindus.[41]

I will never forget my excitement when I first read this. Without doubt, Capra's was an experi-ence of spiritual insight, of mystical depth, that brought together years of study in the area of quantum mechanics with the deepest of mystical traditions. For him, we might say, this was a moment of *enlightenment,* as John Hagelin would see it. The tears that came with this unforeseen "gift," bestowed on him "without any effort... from the depth of consciousness,"[42] were the authentic response to sacred Mystery. His grounding in physics provided the framework for articulating what he saw. His fascination for the Hindu mystical tradition gave him the symbols. Perhaps it is in experiences such as this, that we can at last begin to understand and celebrate a clear interface of science and spirituality.

The Tao of Physics was the first book I read many years ago relating the new physics to ancient spiritual traditions. Being a product of the "great divide" between religion and science, but having perhaps been somewhat prepared to accept the ultimate oneness of all human questing for the Holy through my study of, and love for, Martin Heidegger's existential thought,[43] I found in Capra's explorations a powerful invitation to hope.

Mystical Language and Insights

Certainly the spiritual language of Eastern tradition seems, for Capra and others, to lend itself most readily to the worldview emerging in our time as a result of scientific research and discoveries. Capra uses it freely: "Mystics understand the roots of the *Tao* but not its branches, scientists understand its branches but not its roots. Science does not need mysticism and mysticism does not

need science; *but [the human being] needs both.*"[44]
The "interface," then, is necessary for all of us.

Western thinkers and mystics, of course, have their depth insights as well. *The Cloud of Unknowing*, for example, seems to point gently toward Hagelin's unified field centuries before he himself and others espousing the "Field" theory as the "ground" of reality came to that realization. *The Cloud* speaks of "a nature found within all creatures but not restricted to them: outside all creatures, but not excluded from them."[45]

Meister Eckhart speaks in this vein in his time as well, using the religious names to which he was accustomed:

For in the kingdom of heaven all is in all,
all is one and all is ours. And in the kingdom of
heaven everything is in everything else.
All is one and all is ours.
We are all in all as God is all in all.

What if today we replaced Eckhart's imagery with Hagelin's terminology?

For in *the unified field of pure consciousness*
all is in all, all is one and all is ours. And in
the unified field of pure consciousness
everything is in everything else.
All is one and all is ours. We are all in all as

the unified field of pure consciousness
is all in all.

David Bohm's "holomovement" of "unfolding" and "enfolding" seems to resonate with Eckhart's centuries-older words:

All creatures flow and return to their source....
What is created flows out but remains within.

Eckhart touches the *pure vacuum* of contemporary cosmology, the non-visible, pure emptiness characterizing the zero-point field and mysteriously, as well as paradoxically, giving rise to everything that is, when he observes:

All creatures have been drawn from nothingness
and that is why their origin is nothingness.

The mystical (apophatic) language for God clearly supports primordial emptiness, the pure vacuum, no-thingness as the fertile ground for all reality: abyss, darkness, nakedness, wilderness, purity, simplicity, unity—or, as Eckhart says, *"one with One, one from One, one in One, and in One, One everlastingly."* It refers to ultimate Mystery as "unnameable, unknowable, transcendent that continuously recedes beyond reference."[46]

4

LIGHT AND CONSCIOUSNESS

*A time will come when you will empty
out into the universe,
Taking to your heart the light of ages
now and long ago.*
—Jane Marie Thibault

The frequent references in mystical tradition to inner light have Peter Russell (and myself along with him) surmising a close parallel between inner light and the light fascinating contemporary physics. Could there be a fundamental connection between them, he wonders.

The Sufi Abu 'l-Hosian al-Nuri experienced a light *"gleaming in the unseen....I gazed at it continually, until the time came when I had wholly become the light."* A Maitri Upanishad describes it as *"the fire which is in the sun, the fire which is in the earth, that fire is in my own heart."* Saint Symeon in the tenth century reflected on *a light infinite and incomprehensible...one single light... simple, non-composite, timeless, eternal...the source of life.* And for Ralph Waldo Emerson, *"time and space are but physiological colors which the eye makes, but the soul is light."*[47]

Some might call this inner light of the soul "consciousness"—restricted not merely to the mind but present in the entire person. The more Russell explored it, the more he saw its connection to the light of physics which, as the most basic component of all matter (the photon), has no solidity; in fact, has none of the normal "properties" of matter. Were we to use standard dualistic parlance for this insight, we would call this kind of "non-material" essential component of matter *spirit,* and then would find ourselves, to our great amazement, uniting what for millennia has been kept apart.

> Physical light has no mass, and is not part of the material world. The same is true of consciousness; it is immaterial. Physical light seems to be fundamental to the universe. The light of consciousness is likewise fundamental: without it there would be no experience.
>
> I [Russell] began to wonder whether there was some deeper significance in these similarities. Were they pointing to a more fundamental connection between the light of the physical world and the light of consciousness? Do physical reality and the reality of the mind share the same common ground—a ground whose essence is light?[48]

As we are aware, the mystics speak of *enlightenment* or illumination as a heightened form of awareness, a culmination point of wisdom and inner stillness. Ordinary parlance also seems, almost unconsciously, to assume the common ground Russell is seeking. We speak of an intelligent person as *bright* or even *brilliant,* of someone not so gifted as *dull.* When we do not understand something, we implore someone *to shed light on the matter.* When we are uninformed, we plead not *to be kept in the dark.* When consciousness is compromised, a colloquialism refers to the light as *having gone out.* For our collective psyche, then, consciousness and light appear to be one.

In my book *In the Stillness You Will Know,* I referenced Janusz Slawinski's study on light, which claims that dying organisms actually emit intense amounts of light, which he refers to as a "light shout."[49] Not everyone can see this "light shout, " just like most of us cannot ordinarily see the auric field of light always around our bodies. Neither of them seem to be within our ordinary visual range. Hospice nurses, however, have assured me that on occasion they have seen the light leaving their patient's body at the moment of death.

We know, from the above citation by Peter Russell, that consciousness and light seem to have the same characteristics. Neither has shape or place. They are both invisible, but nothing can be recognized or seen without them. Both are independent of space and time. Can it be, then, that beyond merely a fundamental "connection," they are one and the same? Perhaps we simply *are* beings of light, and the familiar citations in scripture referring to us as beings of light are, in fact, beyond the merely symbolic and have their roots in our very essence.

No one affirms this quite as convincingly for me as does Jacques Lusseyran, the hero of the French Resistance during the Second World War who, though totally blinded at eight years of age and without any knowledge of, or experience in, depth meditation, had a continuous sense of inner light, truly visible to him throughout his life. The light that he describes in his autobiography, *And There Was Light,* guided him and, very likely, saved his life during his incarceration in the infamous Buchenwald concentration camp. He was one of only thirty survivors of the original two-thousand French prisoners there.

Lusseyran candidly admits the light vibrations that came to him shortly after his accident had a deeply spiritual dimension, even though they also guided him in his contact with the external world. They turned every sound, smell, and shape into vibrations of light with variations of color. The only time the light would diminish to the point of almost vanishing, he tells us, was when he would allow himself to feel fear and mistrust, anger, ambition, impatience, or jealousy. As long as he embraced his surroundings with trust and love, was serene, and maintained an open confidence toward his surroundings, "he as well as his whole world were bathed in light, as if 'existing through it and because of it.'"[50]

> I was aware of a radiance emanating from a place I knew nothing about, a place which might as well have been outside me as within. But radiance was there, or, to put it more precisely, light....
>
> I felt indescribable relief, and happiness so great it almost made me laugh....I found light and joy at the same moment, and I can say without hesitation that from that time on light and joy have never been separated in my experience....
>
> The amazing thing was that this was not magic for me at all, but reality....I bathed in [light]....I could feel light rising, spreading, resting on objects, giving them form, then leaving them.
>
> Withdrawing or diminishing is what I mean, for the opposite of light was never present....
>
> Light was my whole reason for living. I let it rise in me like water in a well, and I rejoiced.[51]

However one might understand this extraordinary lifelong experience of light described in his book, it is clear that, for Jacques Lusseyran, light was his life force. He "saw" it in his blindness, and through it he encountered the world. Light was in him and through him, as natural as vision is for the sighted. But it did more. It encouraged his sense of community, fed his inner life, and fostered kindness and benevolence.

Lusseyran's was "an experiential reality of light and consciousness that is beyond mathematics and the laboratory as such." His account seems to give us "a sense of something larger, something beyond us that is nevertheless intimately one with us."[52] Our previous discussion of Hagelin's "unified field of pure consciousness" comes to mind, or McTaggart's "quantum sea of light." Perhaps Lusseyran's experience of the light, involving not just physical "vision," but moral and affective "insight" as well, can help us recognize and interpret this "Field" in a more personal sense, seeing its positive influence on us as humans. That this experience was initially given to a child cannot but bring to mind the scriptural observation: "What you have hidden from the wise and intelligent you have revealed to the merest children" (Matt 1:25).

From the purely scientific point of view, the presence to, and influence of, light on a blind person both in the intra- and interpersonal realm seem difficult to explain. Yet the study of photons (packets or waves of light) as primary components of matter—*without* any of the generally accepted properties of matter—makes Lusseyran's experience at least somewhat approachable. "We are multidimensional beings," writes Richard Gerber, MD.

We are more than just flesh and bones, cells and proteins. We are beings in dynamic equilibrium with a universe of energy and light of many different frequencies and forms. We are composed of the stuff of the universe which…is actually frozen light. Mystics throughout the ages have referred to us as beings of light. It is only now that science has begun to validate the basic premise behind this statement.[53]

In an interesting and groundbreaking book, *Light: Medicine of the Future*, optometrist and specialist in syntonics (light therapy) Jacob Liberman makes, I believe, the depth connection we have been struggling with throughout this section:

It is imperative that we "evolve" ourselves, integrating everything that allows us to become whole, more relational, and aware of our global community. Our task is to take in and utilize light so we may merge with our true selves and our destiny, thus facilitating the healing of our planet. As each of us become whole, we radiate light— light from within—unimpeded by our self-imposed emotional and physical blocks. The medicine of the future is light. We are healing ourselves with that which is our essence.[54]

Part II

REFOCUSING THE QUEST

5

OUR SEARCH FOR GOD

Whenever we expand the realm of our experience, the limitations of our rational mind become apparent and we have to modify, or even abandon, some of our concepts. —**Fritjof Capra**

"But how can you relate to God when you start thinking this way? Where is the *personal* God that loves us and answers our prayers?" a friend asked me not long ago, when I was sharing some of the above reflections with her. This clearly is an important question for most religions and certainly for Christianity. Our anthropomorphisms are precious to us and inspire most of our day-to-day spirituality. The silent void of mystical union somehow seems foreign and cold when one wants to pray for divine support and protection. The worldview that is emerging for us will take some getting used to, and for many of us this may not happen immediately, leaving us, therefore, standing with one foot in the old and another, very gingerly, in the new.

Meister Eckhart is said to have prayed "God to rid [him] of God"—to free him from the images that he saw as ultimately pointing away from the Mystery rather than leading to it; and that he saw as distracting, misleading, blinding him to the essence of the Holy, rather than giving him sight. Most of us, I suspect, would prefer to be less radical than Eckhart. Language, after all, is the primary way by which we communicate and relate. We want to use its symbols and metaphors in our discourse about and with God. It may help us, therefore, to remember that the source and ground of any being cannot be less than what springs forth from it. If indeed "we live and move and have our being" in the Holy One as the underlying *sea of creative energy*, the *all-nourishing abyss* holding all that is in its being, then what we are—our body and mind, our freedom, our passion, our search for truth and love, and certainly our precious personhood as well—only can spring from this *quantum sea of light*. "We live and breathe there," McTaggart assures us. All that we are comes from this plenum, expressing love and passion and relational power in and through us and yet being always *so much more*.

We learn from holography that the whole is in each part and yet we know that, paradoxically, it is also always greater than the sum of its parts. In that sense we can say that the fullness of divine Mystery dwells within each of us, empowers us, moves us, holds us in love, and loves through us, and yet is infinitely more, beyond us, transcending all.

At-onement

Still, we might be discouraged by the realization that this Holy Presence, as the *all-nourishing abyss,* also expresses itself in everything else. Our "special-ness" is, therefore, "compromised" with God, as well as in all of creation. That, of course, is true and points us clearly to the moral transformation necessary for an authentic embrace of the emerging worldview. We remember from chapter 2 Teilhard's spirituality of communion and Brian Swimme's "communion event" necessary for a wholehearted entering into, and inhabiting of, the universe. The emerging values for our time in history revolve around community, interconnection, relationality, and love.

The dualistic perspective, which has ruled our self-understanding for so many centuries, valued distinction and, with it, "specialness." We identified ourselves by our differences and treasured them. From them we derived our notions of superiority and inferiority, a sense of better and worse, of inclusion and exclusion, of togetherness and segregation. From them, also, hierarchy was born. Today, however, we are invited toward identity through "at-onement" and interconnectivity. We have no choice, really, for we know now what we did not know before: Nothing happens anywhere in the universe that does not affect everything, everywhere, instantly. It is slowly beginning to dawn on us, therefore, that we need each other and all other creatures; that the good or ill we visit upon each other and all of creation irrevocably will include us also in its sphere of influence. The quantum perspective tells us today that separation is an illusion. We belong to each other. Communion is our essence. "Things and events once conceived as separate," says Danah Zohar, are in fact "so integrally linked that their bond mocks the reality of both space and time. They behave instead as multiple aspects of some larger whole,"[55] which expresses itself through their specific characteristics and also gifts them with meaning. This larger whole holds everything in relationship, and that includes us as individual selves and as persons.

> With a quantum view of the self, and an understanding of the way my own self is literally... woven into the selves of others (has become a pattern on the quantum substrates of their consciousness), my place in this process becomes more personal and more abiding. I am not just a link in the chain of process, a bridge that others cross on the road to the future....
>
> "I," not just my atoms or my genes, but my personal being—the pattern that is me—will be part and parcel of all that is to come, just as it is

part of the nexus of the now and, indeed, was in a large part foreshadowed in the past....

   There is no real division in space or time between selves. We are all individuals, but individuals within a greater unity, a unity that defines each of us in terms of others and gives each of us a stake in eternity.[56]

Spirituality for today, therefore, calls us unquestionably into a community of the Sacred, where the inside and the outside intertwine, where the goodness we saw outside of us and worshipped beyond us for so long, the holiness above us, flows through our veins instead and can be experienced beneath the surface of our very skin. To paraphrase Teresa of Avila: "The Holy One has no body now but ours." Our God, then, is indeed a personal God and calls us to personhood, to sisterhood and brotherhood. God does so by virtue of being creator and ground of everything that is, as well as being experientially through each of us, whose essence and fulfillment is love.

Presence

   Our perceived contact with God could, nevertheless, be seen as compromised with the above considerations. Some could claim that it is one thing to be assured that personhood comes from and is contained in God as the source of everything that is; it is another, however, to connect with this God. So much for us depends on experience and visualization. How does one relate to a *quantum sea of Light*? Even if one were to use theological terms—such as Rahner's "ground of being," or Rudolph Otto's "the holy," or simply the *idea* of "divine source"—how does one *see* this in relation to oneself?

Years ago I meditated on the experience of *presence* as possibly moving us beyond our self-imposed strictures on religious experience.[57] Perhaps it can help us here, once again, and offer the depth connection we are looking for. I reflected on Ralph Harper's approach to the experience of *presence* in his little book entitled simply: *On Presence: Variations and Reflections.* For Harper, *presence* touches us at the root of human experience and easily surpasses the distinctions between sacred and profane, offering a clear and deeply felt opening to the divine. To illustrate what he means, he reflects on art, music, nature, such moments of beauty as being moved by a night sky, "by the soughing of pines in early spring," when the distance disappears between the one who listens and sees, and that which is *there* and gives itself to him or her.[58] In such experiences oneness happens, and its gift is *presence.* To my mind came Rodin's *Kiss,* Dali's *Last Supper,* and the second movement of Beethoven's Triple Concerto. I thought of my first visit to the Black Canyon of the Gunnison in Colorado, of walking through the redwood forest of northern California, of visiting once again the Freiburger Münster in southern Germany—the cathedral of my childhood and a masterpiece of Romanesque and Gothic art.

One feels at ease in moments of *presence,* enveloped by the good. One can breathe deeply, sigh. There is a sense of rightness, of homecoming, of quiet peace and awe. Ecstasy finds its home in *presence*—a moving out and beyond oneself. Monika Hellwig calls these encounters moments of the "most basic and universally available revelation." One discovers "the all-encompassing power and presence of the One who is greater than we are, prior to us, transcending our ability to grasp...the silent but welcoming backdrop to all our experiences of life."[59] And Harper adds:

> When I think of presence, I think of what it is like for the soul to be touched, the mystery of the whole self, body and spirit....Presence can be explosive, liberating, revealing, quieting.... Presence has force and authority....It is a unitary experience and an experience of totality in the midst of shattering differences.[60]

Should one be blessed by the company of others to share a moment such as this, the experience almost always evokes communion. It gifts us with knowledge that surpasses mere mind. "We know that we know that we know," and this knowledge is love. It is brotherhood and sisterhood. It is homecoming, at-onement, in a communal *yes*.

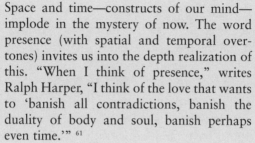

> Space and time—constructs of our mind—implode in the mystery of now. The word presence (with spatial and temporal overtones) invites us into the depth realization of this. "When I think of presence," writes Ralph Harper, "I think of the love that wants to 'banish all contradictions, banish the duality of body and soul, banish perhaps even time.'" [61]

What we feel during experiences such as these does not necessarily require what we commonly understand by a "personal" God in the form, for example, of the Father/Mother, or of the divine Three. *Presence* comes simply, as well as definitively, through a sense of the More, of the quietly and overwhelmingly Deep, of archetypal Mystery. It can evoke tears, a softening of the heart, vulnerability, joy, surrender—not so much to someone, as to the All. One senses timelessness, infinite space. One whispers or exults, prostrates, dances, or simply smiles and closes one's eyes. In every way, *presence* is an encounter beyond understanding. It is holy and manifests the divine.

6

PRAYER

I have arrived, I am home, In the here,
In the now.
I am solid. I am free. In the ultimate
I dwell.
    —Thich Nhat Hanh

I want to believe that depth prayer is a response to *presence*. As such, I see it more as a dwelling *in*, than a kneeling *before* the Holy. It grows out of inwardness and wonder, with few words, and often with a deep and overwhelming, as well as ever-growing, awareness of inner power and light.* This awareness comes from an acknowledged connectedness to the Source and to the energy that flows through the universe and centers in us as the

---

    * Prayer can, of course, also arise through longing *for* the More and a waiting in the face of what feels like emptiness and a sense of desolation. I suspect, however, that even what may appear as "desolation" could not happen without there having been a prior experience of *presence*.

place where the flow can be channeled, utilized for healing, and celebrated.

In this context, the sense of God as the great provider does not fit well any longer, and prayers of petition become rare and eventually may even cease. We send light or love energy instead. We silently hold another in our hearts, connected as they are to the Love that is God in the universe, and we know that good will come of it. The God who meets us in the worldview of the twenty-first century touches us from within the universe, in its unfolding—a holy event that blesses all of creation and intimately involves us.

In a previous section, "Adjusting Our God Space," we reflected already on the de-literalization necessary in this regard. Without denying a deep sense of the More and of the Transcendent, there needs to be in today's person of prayer a profound sense of belonging, of experiencing "I in You and You in me," and of moving away from notions of unworthiness, distance, and separation. This prayerful sense of belonging is based on trust in the cosmic benevolence that surrounds us, cherishes us, sustains us; that effects wholeness, healing, and well-being, and does so in and through us. Gratitude and rejoicing, rather than petition and pleading, may be the more appropriate dispositions here.

> Transcending the ordinary sequence of time, we are grateful for achieving what we hope for, and we dwell in trust, allowing benevolence to unfold.

Numerous motivational speakers today, appealing to every imaginable audience, speak to this insight by evoking the "power of intention," the "power of attraction," the "power of thought"—insisting that thought is energy and can effect what it envisions.

It always surprises me when I observe how eagerly business seems to be embracing this theme, and I am equally disappointed that spirituality tends to be much slower on the uptake. Recently on a flight home from a seminar I had given, I saw the gentleman seated next to me engrossed in Eckhart Tolle's *The Power of Now.* When the opportunity presented itself, I asked him what interested him in the book and discovered to my amazement that he was contracted by companies to help increase productivity in the workforce. He was reading the book in search of new ideas. Tolle's book is a mystical reflection on what contemporary science might see as the space time continuum. The companies hiring my traveling companion were hoping to reverse the fact that many of us allow ourselves to be unduly victimized and disempowered by the flow of time; thus, in a deeper sense, we "never really are where we are." We worry about the future; we regret and despise, mourn or romanticize the past; we ignore the present. This, among other things, negatively affects productivity and hurts business.

It also weakens the power of prayer. The energy that could be focused on the present moment is dissipated by our dwelling on the past or dreaming ahead into the future. We have seen already ("Lessons Learned from Light" and "Wisdom of Scientists and Mystics") that time is a construct of our particular mode of consciousness. Truly being in the *here* and *now* (experiencing *presence* and *present*) concentrates the power flowing through us, enhances our effectiveness, and expands consciousness beyond space and time, eliminating our separateness and connecting us back to the Source. This is essential for concentration of thought and, therefore, extremely valuable for prayer.

Allowing Energy to Flow

For participants in my classes, these concepts appear to be difficult to grasp. Somehow, touching into the power within does not seem to be something we are used to. Petitioning the God above still seems to be our safest route if we want to effect change through prayer. There is resistance, therefore, to the numerous experiments by scientists these days testing the effectiveness of healing prayer. In a recent class I taught on "Spirituality and the New Science," the notion of control groups in such experiments seemed particularly offensive to the participants. "God does not pick and choose at random," they claimed. It seemed to them cruel to use human beings as test subjects in such a way. They felt that it presented God as capricious, an image not worthy of God.

It took me some time to help them see that what was being tested was not God's "mood," or arbitrary choosing, but the effectiveness of those who prayed—their capacity, in other words, to tap into the love energy in the universe and send healing through their focused intention. For many of us, God still seems to be "outside," listening to our petitions, granting them when "he" sees fit. We remember the statement: "God answers all our prayers, but sometimes the answer is no."

 It is difficult for us to grasp that we are the channels of love and healing, by virtue of our very being here as creation-come-to-consciousness-and-love.

We are channels of peace and goodwill. When we pray to God "out there" to bestow peace on a world torn by war, we betray our role and abdicate our power—holy power flowing through us and throughout the universe. The creative energy in the universe is focused in us by virtue of the freedom and consciousness that make us who we are. It can be used for good and ill as noted in an earlier section, "Call to Transformation." Thoughts of divisiveness and hate increase the power of war. Thoughts of benevolence and reconciliation help bring about peace.

A 1993, two-month study conducted by the National Demonstration Project in Washington, DC, showed the effect of transcendental meditation on violence in that city:

> When the local…group increased to 4000, violent crime, which had been steadily increasing during the first five months of the year, began to fall, to 24 percent, and continued to drop until the end of the experiment. As soon as the group disbanded, the crime rate rose again. The study demonstrated that the effect couldn't have been due to such variables as weather, the police or any special anti-crime campaign.[62]

Studies of group prayer seem to indicate that the critical mass required for transformation is really very small—a mere 1 percent of the population involved. Christiane Northrup, MD, suggests that in order to enhance the power for peace in the world, we must create virtual peace scenarios in our minds—envisioning an end to the Iraq war,[63] for example, or seeing Darfur free of ethnic cleansing. We could then send these images into the universe, accompanied with blessings and thanksgiving.

It is important to remember that there is really no one method of prayer that proves to be superior to others. Fred Sicher and Elisabeth Targ's group of healers, over a six-month period of healing prayer, significantly influenced the health condition of end-stage AIDS patients; these healers represented every imaginable variety of prayer styles and religious orientations: Christians, Buddhists, Jewish kabbalists, practitioners from nonreligious healing schools, contemplatives, Evangelicals, a Sioux shaman, a *Qigong* master, a Catholic who recited the Rosary. Their only common element was their firm conviction and previous success in healing through prayer.[64]

I would surmise that in the healing practice of Jesus, his own strong sense of God's presence in and through him, coupled with the power of trust present in those who came to him for healing, were key as well. His exhortation, "Go in peace. Your faith has made you whole," and his inability to heal in his hometown because of the people's lack of faith, seem to attest to this. Interconnectivity and action at a distance seemed to have worked equally in the healings of Jesus, for he did not seem to consider his physical presence essential (Matt 8:13). It also worked in the healing experiment of Fred Sicher and Elisabeth Targ, for their diverse group of healers were spread throughout the country.

As we have seen, time and space are transcended by consciousness. They are transcended by prayer as well. Successful experiments at Stanford University and elsewhere proving the efficacy of "action at a distance" and psychic abilities both forward and backward in time[65] now give us some understanding of prayer related to the healing of memories, as well as to ancestral healing. Furthermore, if our sense of the "hereafter" has moved us beyond an actual place of reward and punishment, and if consciousness, the light that we are, transcends time and space, we might consider the human passage after death as simply a movement into another dimension, another mode of being, that remains somehow connected to us and is open to influence from us and vice versa. Prayer can move us there, and benevolence can be effective either way. The ancients were sensitive to this reality and so is our Christian devotion to the Communion of Saints. Our present reflections simply add the possibility of mutuality by virtue of what we now know about nonlocal and transtemporal interconnectivity.

 The meeting point between science and spirituality is consciousness. As Peter Russell observes: "When science sees consciousness to be a fundamental quality of reality, and religion takes God to be the light of consciousness shining within us all, the two worldviews start to converge."[66]

7

CHRIST JESUS

The Christian understanding of incarnation is not just about a coming of God in the flesh of humanity, but also about the transformation of our biological condition into one more transparent to the power of the spirit.
—Diarmuid O'Murchu

No reflection on the interface of science and spirituality in a Christian setting, such as Saint Mary's College and the Madeleva Lecture series, would be complete without at least some thought given to the place of Christ Jesus in the emerging worldview. I realize that the scope of this lecture does not permit any lengthy discussion of this topic; that brevity, on the other hand, runs the risk of superficiality. I do believe, however, that there are a number of issues that can be raised regarding this primary love and energy source of our faith, and so I want to at least touch on some and open them up for reflection.

We know Jesus of Nazareth was a historical person, a human being who lived his convictions even to the point of death. He bore witness in his time and context to a God of compassion and unconditional forgiveness. He healed and exorcised. He rejected violence and included public outcasts in his table-fellowship. He stood, as Walter Wink would insist, for a domination-free order.[67] As Christians we believe, furthermore, that God emerged most fully in Jesus. By faith, we hold that Jesus the Christ makes God present to us. Or, as Roger Haight would put it, that "it is no less than God with whom we are confronted in Jesus."[68]

The Emergence of God in Humanity

There are some exciting considerations concerning the above observations that invite our attention. To begin with, our emphasis today, in distinction from theological perspectives of the past, might be most effectively placed on the witness that Jesus gave to God as a *human being*. We believe that in him, in his life lived with integrity, the God that empowers all of creation, and is the love, life, and light that flows through the universe, emerged and expressed divinity to the fullest. Taking in the power of this insight (something, I believe, that can happen only slowly and with deliberate attention) brings to our awareness that we, since we are human too, are therefore also called to this emergence, called to the truth and integrity and holiness of our humanity. The life of Jesus was the "presencing" of God. Ours is called to be that as well, as we embrace the fullness of our humanity and walk into the Christ-story that becomes paradigmatic, a saving grace for all of us. The implications here are stupendous.

What we meditate on when we read the Christian scriptures, then, is not only *his* story as such, the events of his life as they were recorded for our edification. It is also the story that he lived *for our salvation*. That means it is the totality of his life lived (intentionally, consciously, or not) for *us* to live. Our "entering into his story," today, then, needs to be done in *our* time and *our* context. That is why we call it *our* "salvation story," which in this moment of history is meant to be *our* doing and which effects our salvation that way.

Salvation history is meaningless if we see it as merely historical, that is, events recorded as having happened to Jesus of Nazareth for our admiration and imitation. "Taking on the Christ," instead, is a transhistorical event. We move beyond time and space as we understand them linearly, and *become* the Body. The energy flow for us, in other words, enters the *now,* and the road to Galilee on which he returned to his place of witness after the resurrection event some two-thousand years ago becomes the road we are called to travel today—

each of us, caught up in his vision and for the sake of God's reign "wherever" and "whenever" we are.

> If you want to know what the body of Christ is, hear what the Apostle tells believers: "You are Christ's body and his members" (1 Cor 12:27). If, then, you are Christ's body and his members, it is your symbol that lies on the Lord's altar—what you receive is a symbol of yourself. When you say *Amen* to what you are, your saying it affirms it. You hear [the priest say] "The body of Christ," and you answer "Amen," and you must be the body of Christ to make that *Amen* take effect.   —St. Augustine, Sermon 272

Salvation, as we reflect on it here, therefore, can no longer be seen solely as an isolated event effected some two-thousand years ago through the death and resurrection of Jesus, important though this was. Divinization, also, is more than merely the result of God's incarnation through the Virgin Mary. The history of salvation, rather, extends across the eons of human history and touches all people of goodwill:

- All those who live the vision of compassion, of unconditional forgiveness, of inclusiveness, of love, of respect for neighbor as well as for alien, of acceptance, even celebration, of diversity

- All those who stand for nonviolence and justice and unconditional love, for the peace that Jesus embodied as he was remembered in the stories that celebrate his life here on earth

To embrace his vision and live his story allows for the "presencing" of God among us, for the emerging of God in humankind, for the embodying of the divine—divinization.

The Evolutionary Unfolding of Love

> The day will come when, after harnessing the winds, the tides and gravitation, we shall harness for God the energies of Love. And on that day, for the second time in the history of the world, [humankind] will have discovered fire. —Teilhard de Chardin [69]

In Jesus we encounter the "personal" God, Emmanuel, and all our human needs for personal contact with the Holy One can be satisfied. In Jesus, too, the extraordinary challenge of what it means to be fully human in the cosmic story is brought home to us. If, however, Teilhard was right, and the universe story is indeed the evolutionary unfolding of love, much will still have to be learned by us.

In a previous book, *In the Stillness You Will Know*, I reflected on the encounter between Peter and Jesus after the resurrection (John 21:15–18). Of significance to me was the gentle but persistent inquiry on the part of Jesus about love, and Peter's ardent reply. This is followed by a prediction concerning Peter's death and the suggestion that God would be glorified therein. What was it in Peter's dying, I wondered, that would glorify God? A simple answer about suffering and expiation no longer spoke to me. The context of our time does not understand a deity demanding sacrifice and decreeing human torture and death. What was it then, both in the death of Jesus, as well as that of Peter, that glorified God?

There is, in the emerging scientific worldview we have been discussing, a possible perspective that could help us deepen our spirituality here by having us see redemption in terms of cosmic reconciliation, healing, and transformation. We might begin by asking ourselves this: whether in the crucifixion of Jesus and in that of Peter; whether in the deaths of Romero and other martyrs for the sake of justice in El Salvador, in Liberia, and in Brazil; whether in all such events— *love*, the highest expression of cosmic energy, met the challenge of its opposite, met hate, callous indifference, and cruelty, embraced them nonjudgmentally, and thus redeemed them through transformation.

It seems that the cosmic story—the living, changing, dynamic universe we live in—unfolds

72

that way, evolves in the dialectic encounter and mutual conversion of opposites, of matter and antimatter. This encounter always brings with it annihilation followed by radical transformation. In the subatomic world, for example, when an electron encounters a positron (its antiparticle), both of them destroy each other, but in their place appear two photons (light), "which instantly depart the scene at the speed of light."[70] The macrocosm has similar occurrences, particularly, some maintain, in the formation of quasars,[71] leading Diarmuid O'Murchu to observe that, in all of creation from the subatomic to macrocosmic reality, "Calvary precedes resurrection; darkness gives way to light."[72]

Could it be, then, that the glory of God that we are wondering about unfolds in the evolutionary love-process of creation itself? Expressed at its deepest, and reaching its full consciousness in Jesus and through all the martyrs for justice after him, could it be that this love embraces its opposite in total freedom and compassion and submits without hesitation to the suffering that this entails for the sake of healing and growth? Is this the love we are called to, a love moving toward ever-deeper reconciliation, involving us intimately and ultimately in the redemptive process of changing darkness into light?

"Forgive seventy times seven times."

"Do good to those who hate you."

"Turn the other cheek."

"Love one another."

If this is so, then the love-transformation that is asked of us as the universe-come-to-consciousness is indeed challenging. Teilhard may have been right when he compared it to humankind's discovery of fire—to our creation of light.

 If the transformation of consciousness that the interface of science and spirituality is moving toward can, however, open us even just a little bit in that direction, humankind will, indeed, have taken a major step toward divinization.

NOTES

1. Marcus Borg, *Jesus: A New Vision: Spirit, Culture, and the Life of Discipleship* (New York: Harper Collins Publishers, 1991), 79.

2. The story of Fritz-Albert Popp as recounted by Lynne McTaggart, *The Field: The Quest for the Secret Force of the Universe* (New York: Quill, Harper Collins, 2003), 39–55, is a good example of this. His position at the University of Marburg, Germany, was compromised because of his research into biophoton emissions.

3. Bruce Lipton, PhD, *The Biology of Belief: Unleashing the Power of Consciousness, Matter and Miracles* (Santa Rosa, CA: Mountain of Love/Elite Books, 2005), 16.

4. Brian Swimme, *The Hidden Heart of the Cosmos: Humanity and the New Story* (Maryknoll, NY: Orbis, 1996), 71, 72.

5. Ibid., 71.

6. Ibid., 85–86.

7. Ibid., 87.

8. Ibid., 87, 88.

9. Ibid., 93.

10. Ibid.

11. McTaggart, 19.

12. Ibid.

13. Ibid., 23, 24.

14. Ibid., 21.

15. Ibid., 24.

16. The word *symbol* itself even seems to be suspect, as the recent silencing of Roger Haight, author of *Jesus Symbol of God* (Maryknoll, NY: Orbis, 1999) painfully illustrates.

17. Peter Russell, *From Science to God: A Physicist's Journey into the Mystery of Consciousness* (Novato, CA: New World Library, 2002), 63.

18. Ibid., 64.

19. Ibid.

20. Ibid., 56, citing Kant.

21. Ibid., 42, citing Schrödinger.

22. Swimme, 100.

23. Ervin Laszlo, *Science and the Akashic Field: An Integral Theory of Everything* (Rochester, VT: Inner Traditions, 2004), 140.

24. Ibid., 2, italics added.

25. Michael Talbot, *The Holographic Universe* (New York: Harper Collins, 1991), 46.

26. The holographic "film is an implicate order because the image encoded in its interference patterns is a hidden totality enfolded throughout the whole. The hologram projected from the film is an explicate order because it presents [three-dimensionally] the unfolded and perceptible version of the image." Ibid., 47.

27. Ibid.

28. Russell, 34, italics added.

29. Dolphins, for example, taking in the human

body do not experience solidity but perceive something akin to an ultrasound scan. Ibid., 51, 52.

30. Ibid., 50.

31. Ibid., 48, 49.

32. Swimme, 101.

33. Teilhard de Chardin as discussed by Beatrice Bruteau, *The Grand Option: Personal Transformation and a New Creation* (Notre Dame, IN: University of Notre Dame Press, 2001), 1–3, quotation on p. 3

34. Barbara Fiand, *From Religion Back to Faith: A Journey of the Heart* (New York: Crossroad, 2006), 65.

35. Aniella Jaffé, *The Myth of Meaning: Jung and the Expansion of Consciousness* (New York: Penguin Books, 1075), 34–36. Cites Lincoln Barnett from *The Universe and Dr. Einstein,* 1950; James Jeans from F. Dessauer's foreword to B. Bavink, *Die Naturwissenschaft auf dem Wege zur Religion;* W. Heitler from *Der Mensch und die naturwissenscaftliche Erkenntnis;* A. Portmann from "Gestaltung als Lebensvorgang," in: *Eranos-Jahrbuch 1960.*

36. Arthur Stanley Eddington, cited by Ken Wilber, *Quantum Questions: Mystical Writings of the World's Great Physicists* (Boston: Shambala Publications, 1984), 10.

37. Wilber, 3–11.

38. Ibid., 9.

39. Russell, 127.

40. For a clear and concise discussion on the phenomenon of atheism see William A. Luijpen and Henry J. Koren, *Religion and Atheism* (Pittsburgh: Duquesne University Press, 1971).

41. Fritjof Capra, *The Tao of Physics* (New York: Bantam Books, 1977), xv.

42. Ibid., xvi.

43. Heidegger's a philosophical approach is fascinating to, among others, both the physicists and Eastern thinkers of the mid-twentieth century.

44. Fritjof Capra, *The Tao of Physics: 25th Anniversary Edition* (Boston: Shambala Publications, 1999), 306.

45. Cited by Russell, 31.

46. Michael Sells on Eckhart, in Paul A. Dietrich, "The Wilderness of God in Hadewijch and Meister Eckhart and His Circle," in *Meister Eckhart and the Beguine Mystics*, ed. Bernard McGinn (New York: Continuum, 1997), 37; italics added.

47. Maitri Upanishad 6:17. The rest are from Russell: al-Nuri, 70; Symeon, 70; Emerson, 82.

48. Russell, 70, 71.

49. Janusz Slawinski, cited in Barbara Fiand, *In the Stillness You Will Know* (New York: Crossroad, 2002), 24.

50. Jacques Lusseyran, cited in Barbara Fiand, *From Religion Back to Faith*, 128.

51. Jacques Lusseyran, *And There Was Light* (New York: Parabola Books, 1998), 16–18.

52. Fiand, *From Religion Back to Faith*, 130, 131.

53. Richard Gerber, MD, *Vibrational Medicine* (Rochester, VT: Bear & Company, 2001), 67.

54. Jacob Liberman, OD, PhD, *Light: Medicine of the Future* (Rochester, VT: Bear & Company, 1991), xxii.

55. Danah Zohar, *The Quantum Self: Human*

Nature and Consciousness Defined by the New Physics (New York: Quill/William Morrow, 1990), 34.

56. Ibid., 151.

57. Barbara Fiand, *Embraced by Compassion: On Human Longing and Divine Response* (New York: Crossroad, 1993), 110–12.

58. Ralph Harper, *On Presence: Variations and Reflection* (Philadelphia: Trinity Press International, 1991), 6.

59. Monika Hellwig, *Understanding Catholicism* (New York: Paulist Press, 1981), 17.

60. Harper, 6, 7.

61. Ibid., 6.

62. McTaggart, 211, from J. S. Hagel et al., "Effects of group practice of the Transcendental Meditation Program on preventing violent crime in Washington, DC: results of the National Demonstration Project, June–July, 1993," *Social Indicators Research,* 1994; 47:153–201.

63. See www.drnorthrup.com/newsletter.php.

64. McTaggart, 188, 189.

65. For numerous accounts of experiments with nonlocal and transtemporal consciousness and spiritual healing, see Russell Targ and Jane Katra, PhD, *Miracles of Mind: Exploring Nonlocal Consciousness and Spiritual Healing* (Novato, CA: New World Library, 1999).

66. Russell, 116.

67. Walter Wink, *The Human Being: Jesus and the Enigma of the Son of Man* (Minneapolis: Fortress Press, 2002), 14.

68. Roger Haight, *Jesus Symbol of God* (Maryknoll, NY: Orbis Books, 1999), 338.

69. Cited in Russell, 129.

70. Gary Zukav, *The Dancing Wu Li Master: An Overview of the New Physics* (New York: Bantam Books, 1980), 211.

71. Quasars are quasi-stellar radio sources, most of which "are only several times the diameter of our solar system, yet emit more energy than an entire galaxy of over 150 billion stars." Ibid., 186.

72. Diarmuid O'Murchu, *Quantum Theology* (New York: Crossroad, 1997), 127.

The Madeleva Lecture in Spirituality

This series, sponsored by the Center for Spirituality, Saint Mary's College, Notre Dame, Indiana, honors annually the woman who as president of the college inaugurated its pioneering graduate program in theology, Sister M. Madeleva, C.S.C.

1985
Monika K. Hellwig
Christian Women in a Troubled World

1986
Sandra M. Schneiders
Women and the Word

1987
Mary Collins
Women at Prayer

1988
Maria Harris
Women and Teaching

1989
Elizabeth Dreyer
Passionate Women: Two Medieval Mystics

1990
Joan Chittister, OSB
Job's Daughters

1991
Dolores R. Leckey
Women and Creativity

1992
Lisa Sowle Cahill
Women and Sexuality

1993
Elizabeth A. Johnson
Women, Earth, and Creator Spirit

1994
Gail Porter Mandell
Madeleva: One Woman's Life

1995
Diana L. Hayes
Hagar's Daughters

1996
Jeanette Rodriguez
Stories We Live
Cuentos Que Vivimos

1997
Mary C. Boys
Jewish-Christian Dialogue

1998
Kathleen Norris
The Quotidian Mysteries

1999
Denise Lardner Carmody
An Ideal Church: A Meditation

2000
Sandra M. Schneiders
With Oil in Their Lamps

2001
Mary Catherine Hilkert
Speaking with Authority

2002
Margaret A. Farley
Compassionate Respect

2003
Sidney Callahan
Women Who Hear Voices

2004
Mary Ann Hinsdale, IHM
Women Shaping Theology

[No Lecture in 2005]

2006
Susan A. Ross
For the Beauty of the Earth

[No Lecture in 2007]